JOY AND TYRANNY

Arnold Wesker

JOY AND TYRANNY

Arias and variations on the theme of violence

OBERON BOOKS
LONDON

WWW.OBERONBOOKS.COM

First published by Oberon Books Ltd in 2011.

521 Caledonian Road, London N7 9RH

Tel: +44 (0) 20 7607 3637 / Fax: +44 (0) 20 7607 3629

e-mail: info@oberonbooks.com

www.oberonbooks.com

A catalogue record for this book is available from the British Library.

ISBN: 978-1-84943-108-8

Cover image: Goya, Francisco de Lucientes, *The 3rd of May 1808, 1814. Executions of Spanish rebels by Napoleon's army on Mountain of Prince Pius outside Madrid* © The Art Archive / Museo del Prado Madrid.

The man that hath no music in himself,
Nor is not moved with concord of sweet sounds,
Is fit for treasons, stratagems and spoils;
The motions of his spirit are dull as night
And his affections dark as Erebus:
Let no such man be trusted.

Shakespeare, *The Merchant of Venice*

'The oldest and most obsessive vision or ideal is that of the perfect society on earth, wholly just, wholly happy, offering a final solution of all human problems within men's grasp, but for one – some one major obstacle such as class war, or the destructive aspects of materialism or of Western technology; or the evil consequences of institutions – state or church; or some other false doctrine or wicked practice – one great barrier but for which the ideal is realised.

It follows that since all that is needed is the removal of this one great obstacle in the path of mankind, no sacrifice can be too great, if only by this means can the goal be attained.

No conviction has caused more violence, oppression, suffering. The cry that the real present must be sacrificed to an attainable ideal future – this demand has been used to justify massive cruelties...'

Extract from speech of acceptance by Sir Isaiah Berlin
on receiving the Jerusalem Prize, May 1979.

Please note this is a pre-rehearsal text. A later text resulting from a production may differ slightly from this current one.

Characters

JASON
aged 33, standing as an Independent M.P.

CHRISTOPHER
JASON's brother, aged 31, a lawyer

CLARE
their mother, aged 58

AMANDA
CHRISTOPHER's fiancée, aged 28, a journalist

FREYDA
restaurateur aged about 45

Speakers' Corner Characters

(Note: they do not address our audience but an imaginary one)

COMEDIENNE
aged about 30

DEBATER
aged about 65

LADY BETTY LEMON
aged about 75, in a wheelchair

Various offstage voices

Settings

A film
A pub bar
Speakers' Corner – three platforms
A restaurant, table for two
A journalist's desk
Clare's bedroom

The EXPLOSION

This is a menacing sound punctuating the flow of the scenes.

Each takes on a different degree of intensity depending where placed. A preliminary placing has been indicated but final placing will be decided upon during rehearsal.

It could be the explosive sound of a suicide bomber, or of a bomb placed in the underground or in a restaurant.

The final sound, however, must be terrifying.

Time – the present

Despite that the script is laid out in 'two parts' there should be no interval.

Part One

is a film.

Setting: a comprehensive school playground.

End of day, pupils coming out into playground.

Two of them meet and stop to chat.

BOY ONE is the slighter, more anxious of the two.

BOY TWO is bright-eyed, confident, long-haired, self-assured in tone and gesture.

BOY ONE: Just twenty-four hours to go!

BOY TWO: Stop counting or the hours won't pass.

BOY ONE: What time does the record shop open?

BOY TWO: 10 a.m. probably.

BOY ONE: We can sleep outside to be the first.

BOY TWO: We can't sleep outside Harum Records, not in Crouch End. The police will think we're up to no good.

BOY ONE: I can't wait.

BOY TWO: Stop fretting, we'll be the first ones there to buy copies.

BOY ONE: Never! Everyone will want the new Led Zeppelin.

BOY TWO: Stop fretting I tell you!

BOY ONE: (*Fretting.*) *Physical Graffiti.* Wonder what it sounds like.

BOY TWO: A double album, bound to have good tunes in it.

BOY ONE: It can't be better than 'Houses of the Holy'.

BOY TWO: But if it is, it'll be bloody amazing.

BOY ONE: How about the Kubric film tomorrow night?

BOY TWO: 2001? Seen it! Twice! Best film ever.

> *Two other kids, BULLIES, approach the two chatting.*
>
> *On 'best film ever' one of the BULLIES kicks BOY TWO from behind.*

Clever!

> *BULLY turns on him menacingly.*

BULLY: Get lost!

BOY TWO: (*Fearlessly.*) OK, I will.

> *But doesn't move.*

(*To BOY ONE.*) So where were we?

BOY ONE: Two thousand and one.

BOY TWO: Oh, yes. The Kubric film.

BULLY: (*Furious to be ignored.*) I said get fucking lost.

BOY TWO: You didn't say 'get *fucking* lost'. You just said '*get lost*', and I said '*ok, I will*'.

BULLY: Move then.

BOY TWO: When I'm ready. I'm talking to my friend here. Do you mind?

BULLY: Yeah, I do mind. You talk too much.

BOY TWO: How can one talk *too* much?

BULLY: Talk too much, smile too much, posh too much.

BOY TWO: '*Posh* too much'??!!!.

BULLY: There you go. Fucking know-all!

BOY TWO: I don't know all, just some. And I can't un-educate myself, not even for you. Sorry, but that's me.

BULLY: And this is me.

> *BULLY smashes a straight-from-the-shoulder fist into BOY TWO's eye.*

> *NOTE: it is important that the offending arm is filmed moving horizontally to its target because the arm must mix and morph – filmically – into the aeroplane crashing into the TWIN TOWERS, just as the bone thrown in jubilation into the air by the victorious ape in Kubrick's '2001' morphs into a space ship.*

> *The Kubrick images link across eons from a first simple thought (the bone as weapon) to a complex one (the space ship).*

> *Our images link the BULLY's spiteful action to the murderous spiteful action of the TWIN TOWER DESTROYERS, suggesting that both actions spring from an adolescent-like inferiority complex.*

> *The BOY TWO's cleverness like the skyward thrusting towers, intimidates those who imagine that only violence, death, and destruction can assuage their frustration, can make the world behave as they want it to behave.*

> *FILM ENDS.*

SCENE 2

A PUB BAR.

CHRISTOPHER and JASON.

CHRISTOPHER: When did you start hating me?

JASON: From the beginning. When I was two years old and happy and then you came along and usurped my place in the scheme of things.

CHRISTOPHER: That's understandable. What's not understandable is why you never got over it. Why did it persist, this hatred?

JASON: Because you didn't stop draining my happiness. You were cleverer than me, better at sports, better looking.

CHRISTOPHER: But you possessed charm. Everyone loved your sweetness. We were a family full of love.

JASON: Ah! Family! Full of love!

CHRISTOPHER: Isn't that what you experienced?

JASON: What I experienced was the tyranny of family love!

CHRISTOPHER: Not tyranny, our parents were disappointed perhaps. They wanted to see us involved in the arts but you chose politics and I chose law.

JASON: The tyranny of expectations, then.

CHRISTOPHER: They couldn't have been really disappointed by our choices whatever their expectations.

JASON: You didn't feel the disappointments, I did.

CHRISTOPHER: That was your problem not the family's.

JASON: Family! Family! *You can't hate him, he's your brother. Your flesh and blood!* What an absurd notion. Just because we were baked in the same oven doesn't mean we had to share the same feelings. There's nothing inherent in the notion of family that guarantees love. Nothing! Go back to the beginning of it all, God himself wanted us to know that family does not equal love.

CHRISTOPHER: Cain and Abel?

JASON: Yes, brother, Cain and Abel. Why did God have Cain kill Abel? We had to learn it at school: '*Cain brought of the fruit of the ground an offering to the Lord…but unto Cain and his offering he had not respect.*' Why? Why was Abel's offerings of '*firstlings of his flock and the fat thereof*' more acceptable to the Lord than Cain's '*fruit of the ground*'? Why was Abel beloved of the Lord and Cain not? Explain it to me. The Bible offers no explanation. '*If thou dost well*' said the Lord, '*shalt thou not be accepted?*' But Cain did well. He was a tiller of the ground and offered the fruit thereof. What is so unacceptable about the fruit of the ground? Wheat, barley, corn, olives…? Of course Cain was angry. Who wouldn't be?

CHRISTOPHER: Enough to murder your brother?

JASON: In some circumstances? Yes!

CHRISTOPHER: Good Lord! What kind of political policies will *you* be promoting to win votes?

JASON: Honesty! The truth of things. Family is *not* the basic unit of civilised society, intelligence is. Stupidity is the offence. And sentimentality.

CHRISTOPHER: Sentimentality?

JASON: Dishonest feelings. Feelings that encourage you to fall in love with yourself.

CHRISTOPHER: I don't believe you can do good *unless* you fall a little in love with yourself.

JASON: But not fall in love with yourself falling in love.

CHRISTOPHER: And Abel did, you think!

JASON: Abel, for sure – cleverer, better at sports, better looking.

CHRISTOPHER: But you can't know that for sure.

JASON: I can safely assume, though.

CHRISTOPHER: Safely! Sunny, self-satisfied, and smiling too much, the tyranny of family joy.

Long pause.

CHRISTOPHER: You know mother is dying?

JASON: How could I not know!

CHRISTOPHER: And it's her birthday in a few weeks time.

JASON: That I had forgotten. What are we buying her?

CHRISTOPHER: She told me what she wants.

JASON: That's the surprise taken out of the gift.

CHRISTOPHER: I don't want surprises, she said. I want what I want.

JASON: And what does she want?

CHRISTOPHER: A painting.

JASON: A painting?

CHRISTOPHER: I have no need for jewellery now, she said, and I've got enough clothes to last me until I die, so I want something to please my eyes. She said it in French: *pour fait plaisir aux yeux.*

JASON: So we have to go traipsing around galleries?

CHRISTOPHER: No, she knows the painting she wants.

JASON: Which is?

CHRISTOPHER: Do you know the shop in Hampstead on the right, leading up to the White Stone Pond? It's full of antiques and oddities.

JASON: I know it. I pass it every day on my way down to Hampstead underground, and I hate it. It's full of the past, a faded past – Victorian shawls, Meissen figurines, silver sugar tongs that no one uses anymore. I can't bear such shops, full of nostalgia for an ugly past. There surely couldn't have been anything there *pour faire plaisir aux yeux.*

CHRISTOPHER: But there was. A painting by Mark Wayner.

JASON: Mark who?

CHRISTOPHER: Wayner. He was part of the Gertler/Bomberg group of East End Jewish painters. They made it but somehow he didn't.

JASON: I saw it! A painting of dancing Jews. It was in the window for ages and then it wasn't and I thought thank Christ it was sold and I didn't have to look at it any more on my way to the office. What on earth does she want to look at dancing Jews for?

CHRISTOPHER: They're called Hassidim.

JASON: I hope she's not thinking of becoming a Hebrew.

CHRISTOPHER: Don't be stupid, Jason.

JASON: Hated it! Dancing for joy – ugh! And the colours were all wrong, dowdy greens and shitty browns. What made mother choose such a painting?

CHRISTOPHER: Ask her when we give it to her.

JASON: I hope you've secured it then.

CHRISTOPHER: Why? There's no hurry. It's been around for ages.

JASON: You never know. Just because she wants it someone else will come along, or there'll be a gas leak and the shop will burn down.

CHRISTOPHER: But –

JASON: (*Snapping.*) BUY IT!

CHRISTOPHER: JASON?

JASON: I'm sorry.

CHRISTOPHER: Why are you snapping?

JASON: Remember what the priest told his congregation: if you want to make God laugh tell him your plans for tomorrow.

SCENE 3

SPEAKERS' CORNER – HYDE PARK.

Speakers are identified by a board flown in.

Board saying COMEDY.

COMEDIENNE: Time – 1923. Place – Soviet Union, carriage of a train from Moscow to Leningrad. Little old Jew huddled in a corner of a compartment, retreating, anxious, clasping a bag to his bosom.

Enter a Soviet General. Train departs. Long, anxious silence. Finally the Soviet General turns to the Jew and asks:

'What makes you Jews so clever?' The little old Jew doesn't want to enter into a long philosophical exchange, and replies simply:

'Herrings!'

'Herrings?'

'Herrings, yes, herrings.' More silence. The Jew unwraps his parcel, takes out a crust of bread and some herrings and begins to eat.

The General can't resist and asks the Jew can he sell him a couple of herrings.

'Of course!' says the Jew.

'How much?' asks the General.

'Three kopeks each,' says the Jew. The General agrees and the kopeks and herrings change hands.

After a minute or so the General stops eating.

'Here!' he cries out. 'Wait a minute! Didn't I see herrings in the market this morning selling for one kopek each?'

'You see,' says the Jew, 'it's working already!'

She hangs over her audience, waiting for applause.
It doesn't come.

EXPLOSION

SCENE 4

A NEWSPAPER OFFICE.

AMANDA is reading out from her computer to a colleague off stage.

AMANDA: Listen to this just coming through. *(Reads.)* '*At least 250 doctors, professors, writers and teachers, the cream of the intellectuals who could have helped create the state were found murdered in a field outside the capital. All had their hands tied behind their backs and had been bayoneted, garrotted or shot*'.

SCENE 5

SPEAKERS' CORNER

COMEDY.

COMEDIENNE: I see you don't like my jokes. Women can't
be funny, you think. Only men know how to laugh at life.
Women take life too seriously, you think.

OK. Let's play a game instead. Let's divide the world.
Example: I believe the world is divided into those who
applaud achievement and those who begrudge it. (*Pause.*)
Another? I believe the world is divided into those who
destroy and those who build. (*Pause.*) Not impressive
enough? Want another? I believe the world is divided into
those who think and those who hate thinkers.

I'll see you next Sunday and I'll expect you to come with
your own divisions. You hear me at the back there?

SCENE 6

A NEWSPAPER OFFICE.

AMANDA: (*Still reading.*) '*The most horrific episode carried out by
the guerrillas of this newly formed state took place when a rally
ended with prayers. There were five prisoners trussed up whose
crime was alleged to have been an attempt to abduct two women.
The crowd began to beat the trussed up men until a group of
the guerrillas wearing black uniforms, pushed them back, fixed
bayonets and began to charge the prisoners themselves. They
stabbed them through the neck, the chest, the stomach, and shot
one of the prisoners with a sten gun. The crowd watched and
the photographers snapped away. A small boy of ten, the son of
one of the prisoners, cradled the head of his dying father, which
infuriated the crowd who trampled the child to death.*'

Damn them!

V. OFF STAGE: You're a journalist, why are you so shocked?

Long, long pause.

AMANDA: Because I want to murder the murderers. Murder them!

EXPLOSION

SCENE 7

SPEAKERS' CORNER.

DEBATE.

DEBATER: My topic for this afternoon is 'Violence'. Violence! Violence! Violence! Everyone's talking about violence – a big mystery! What causes it? Ask me, *I'll* solve the mystery for them.

V. OFF STAGE: We're asking you.

DEBATER: Ever heard of cultural intimidation? Ever met people with *real* inferiority? People who suspect their own stupidity? That's where violence comes from. The anger of self-knowledge. Self-knowledge that they're losers and then – everything intimidates them: a tone of voice, a way of dressing, a passion for literature, a passion for music, for tall buildings, for anything. They hate it! One speck of colour on another's personality unleashes venom, *such* venom.

And the colour is all around – on television, in bookshops, fashion shops, on flamboyant actresses, on protesting students with long hair, black leaders with clenched fists, pop singers, hippies, yippies, Yids! 'Know thyself!' everyone says. 'Unto thine own self be true!' What's that for advice? We *know* ourselves. Only too bloody true we know ourselves. That's the trouble. We know ourselves too well. Can't bear it. Anything that's a deviation from what we are? Hate it! We'll show you who's superior and who's not. Wham!

And there they are, the intimidated, squirming in their factories and offices missing it all. The adverts confirm it. Trapped! All over the place, in little black holes, trapped! Grrrr! Who can I smash? Whose fault is my lousy life? Someone's got to suffer as well as me. Nigger! Artist! Student! Gay! Lynch 'em! Send 'em back! Bring back the gallows, the whip, anything. I-hate-them! I-hate-me! Hate! Grrr! (*Beat.*) Violence? You want to know about violence? Me! Ask *me.*

V. OFF STAGE: What's your authority?

DEBATER: I was a probation officer. You have a question?

SCENE 8

SPEAKERS' CORNER.

LADY BETTY, talks with slight Cockney lilt.

LADY B: My name is Betty Lemon. *Lady* Betty Lemon to be precise, and I'm here to share with you in this crazy world a crazy letter I received the other day. (*Sumptuously.*) Lady Lemon! Ha! He promised he'd become a knight before he died. And he did. Then he died. Honoured and penniless. Though he spent his seed more than his pennies. Philandering bastard! Sir James Lemon! Socialist MP for Birmingham North. Knighted for services rendered to the nation. (*Beat.*) For services rendered at night to the fucking nation, more like!

So this letter. It said – I learned it off by heart, always did have a good memory – it said: *"Dear Lady Lemon. It is with great pleasure that I inform you you have been chosen* – wait for it – *Handicapped Woman Of The Year…'*

Handi-*what* of the year? Me? They telling me there's no one more handicapped in the entire fucking universe than me? And they're crowning me for it?

What glorious son of man conceived such blushing laurels, such awesome accolades, such canonization?

Champion Cripple three cheers! Happy Hobbler Of The Year hurrah! The Seasons Paraplegic Princess, pah pom!

The letter went on, relentlessly. Have you noticed, my friends, how relentless stupidity is? It went on: *'As you may know, the Society For The Elderly Handicapped holds an annual dinner at which the Handicapped Woman Of The Year and the Handicapped Man Of The Year each address us for half an hour on how they overcame their handicaps...'*

Who says I over-fucking-came them?

SCENE 9

CLARE's BEDROOM.

CLARE in bed, AMANDA at her side.

CLARE: They're my sons, Amanda, I can't love one more than the other.

AMANDA: No one's asking you to, Clare.

CLARE: I gave them birth, watched them grow, fed them food and learning as their poor father wanted. There was no more I could do with my frail health. My sons were cursed with sick parents.

AMANDA: I know, Clare, I understand.

CLARE: Do you, Amanda? I sometimes wonder. Your passion for Christopher, I feel, blinds you to the virtues and qualities of his brother.

AMANDA: I'm sorry if it appears like that.

CLARE: Their father wanted them to be musicians, you know. He used to play classical music alongside their cots as a soporific in the hope that it would influence their musical taste. It didn't work. Jason grew up hating music and painting and poetry. 'People pretending to be who they're not,' he thinks, 'the arty-farty ones imagining they've been touched by God'.

AMANDA: He enjoys playing the naughty boy.

CLARE: I know. I just hope that's all he enjoys playing.

The man that hath no music in himself,

Nor is not moved with concord of sweet sounds...

...Let no such man be trusted...

Thank God for Shakespeare.

Pause.

AMANDA: He loves me, you know, your son, Jason.

CLARE: But he would never dishonour his brother.

Silence. No comment.

Never, never! I know my sons. Their feelings for one another may be strained, and I may not have been a perfect mother but I established boundaries never to be crossed, and loyalty was one of them. Possibly the most important.

AMANDA: The problem with loyalty is that it's a quagmire of conflicts. Loyalty to what? Family loyalty? National loyalty? Loyalty to principles, values, religious beliefs?

CLARE: Oh, don't, Amanda. I'm too frail.

26

AMANDA: I'm sorry, Clare. Don't they know what it is yet?

CLARE: Old age they say, and all that flesh is heir to.

AMANDA: But surely....?

CLARE: No, no! I don't mind dying of old age. There's something right and natural about the process. (*Pause.*) Not true. There's never anything right about dying. Do *you* know anybody who was prepared to die? Despite all the suffering and the knowledge of suffering and man's inhumanity, everyone wants to go on living – for ever and ever, gloriously.

AMANDA: Not everyone, Clare.

CLARE: No! Not everyone. You're right.

AMANDA: Some know that when they're old they'll become tired and ready to go; or else they grow to despise themselves so much for not being what they thought they were that they become anxious and eager to fade out.

CLARE: But not me, though. Not me. I can't tell you how much I cherish everything. I know there's a lot that's obscene and ugly but it's never been too oppressive, I've always had the capacity not to be too oppressed. In the end there's such sweetness, such joy in hidden places. I want to stay on and not miss anything. I want to stay with you and my two sons, close and warm and happy. Why shouldn't I want that? Every year the world finds something new to offer: another man makes music or carves an impossible shape out of the rocks or assembles a poem. Someone is always rising up, taking wing, and behind him he pulls the rest of us; and I want to be there, for every movement, every sound. Why should I want to die away from all that?

AMANDA: What about those who leave this life with misery in their hearts?

CLARE: The put-downers I call them. Any opportunity they had they enjoyed putting people down. They had a special tone of voice, the kind of voice that rubbed its hands together. I knew them. *'Look at the ocean,'* they cried, *'see what a little thing is man in all that sea.'* And when space rockets came they had a real ball. *'Look at all those stars. How insignificant is man now!'* Instead of marvelling that man could make it to the moon they found it another opportunity to put him down.

The put-downers! Yeach! Mercifully I have never been one.

SCENE 10

SPEAKERS' CORNER

COMEDY.

COMEDIENNE: Did you know that in Holland during the Nazi occupation the saxophonists in nightclubs were not permitted to sway, and the trumpeters were not allowed to mute their trumpets? Is there anyone of you out there can offer a rationale for such inanity?

Pause.

I believe the world is divided into those who are clever and talented and are massacred, and those who are stupid and do the massacring.

EXPLOSION

SCENE 11

SPEAKERS' CORNER.

LADY BETTY.

LADY B: A handicapped dinner for the handicapped! Didn't go of course. Instead I amused myself by rehearsing the speech I was never going to give.

'My Lords, Ladies and Gentlemen, sound or unsound, firm or infirm, those glowing with health or those ugly with pain. I had an uncle – yes, even old women may once have had uncles – I had an uncle who, recovering from his third heart operation declared to me: '*You think the world is divided into social classes don't you? As a Socialist'* he said, *'you think the big divide in life is between those who have and those who have not. Well let me tell you you are wrong,'* he said. *'The world is divided into those who have health and those who do not have health. That's the only division that counts.'*

Pause.

Was I ever really a socialist?

I called myself one in those days because in those days there was no other name for what I believed. But – ssssh! Don't let on. I never joined! Wasn't a joiner. Couldn't accept majority decisions. Never really liked the majority. Not like Sir James. He loved them. Trod carefully. Loved carefully. Carefully approved of and hated the right people, the marked groups, the listed causes. Not a hair or a word out of place, not a decibel above par, and he clenched his fist very tightly. Me – I took emotional risks, and asked unfashionable questions. Fatal!

And what about those handicapped by demagogues, charlatans, charismatic politicians? What about them?

SCENE 12

CLARE's BEDROOM.

JASON present.

CLARE: Jason, you won't do anything silly with your life will you!

JASON: Trust me, mother.

CLARE: I'm not sure I can.

JASON: I want to stand for Parliament as an Independent, what silliness could be involved in that?

CLARE: I love you, Jason, but I know you.

JASON: Know what about me?

CLARE: You've always been a little wild.

JASON: Wild?

CLARE: Extreme.

JASON: I don't pussyfoot around you mean?

CLARE: Stay away from Amanda.

JASON: You've noticed?

CLARE: So has she. Stay away.

JASON: You know I will but I can't let my feelings not be known.

CLARE: That's been your problem – letting your feelings be known.

JASON: Not all feelings. Some I hold back, but in principle it's not healthy to hold back.

CLARE: But it is healthy to think things through before throwing your feelings around.

JASON: And when you've thought things through and the enemy remains?

CLARE: What enemy? You invent enemies.

JASON: We don't invent enemies we identify them.

CLARE: We! We! That group you hang out with, with your clenched fists in the air. Be different. You're standing as an Independent MP, you should want to be different.

JASON: I hate it when people want to be different. We're born different, isn't that enough without burdening ourselves with more differences? Why do it? Not for any good reason that's for sure, but just to draw attention to ourself. *'I'm different! I'm different!'* Of course you are, we can see you are, we can hear you are, and when you write your stupid books and plays we can see and read you are. That's what I hate about capitalism, it encourages individuality. *'Look at me! Look at me! Different! I'm different!'*

Strike them down! Away with them – the individualists, away with them! Away! Conformity! Order! That's what the world needs.

CLARE: Your language is so violent.

JASON: Not violent – confrontational. That's what politics is – people confronting each other's views –

CLARE: – but not blowing each other up.

JASON: We don't blow each other up in England, mother, not in England.

EXPLOSION

SCENE 13

CLARE's BEDROOM.

AMANDA at her side.

CLARE: Their father wanted them to be composers but I wanted them to be painters.

The shape of things is what excited me. Every object has a personality – not only a human face but a house; not only a bowl of fruit but a dishevelled bedroom; not only a sleeping animal but a dead tree. Recreating the shape in a way that captured its personality seemed to me a thrilling challenge. Not one I could begin to meet, I discovered. But it left me with a haunting facility – everywhere I looked I could see faces: in clouds where the face kept changing its shape; in branches of trees; in the cracked brickwork of a wall; in shadows, crumpled bed sheets, sat-upon cushions, hanging washing…in everything everywhere – a face.

It was a bit scary at first but then it became a pleasure, something I looked forward to, what would I see today, and where? I felt myself in possession of a unique skill, a privileged gift. I'd point it out to others who mostly couldn't see what I saw, which gave me a faintly superior air which roused their wrath. If they couldn't see it, it couldn't be there. I was imagining things. Well, yes, I suppose I was. How fortunate for me that I could. Irritating for them, however.

AMANDA: Perhaps one of our children, your grandchild, will become a composer.

CLARE: Depends if a passion for music permeates your house.

AMANDA: Oh, it will, it will!

CLARE: Foolish parents, wanting this, that and the impossible-other for their children.

AMANDA: I love watching musicians play, especially on television where they bring you close to their faces. Five playing The Trout Quintet, for example. They share smiles in the middle of playing as though they've said something to each other in a secret language, like women who share the mystery of periods and birth. Intimate! They know what it's like to make music and babies as others don't.

CLARE: Intimidating, sometimes.

AMANDA: And people hate, hate feeling excluded. That's why Jason hates music, it excludes him.

SCENE 14

SPEAKERS' CORNER.

COMEDY.

COMEDIENNE: I believe the world is divided into the fearless and the fearful, into the overfed and the underfed, into the helpless and the determined.

VOICE OFF: What about the dead and the living?

COMEDIENNE: Bit too obvious, friend, but on the right track. Now, guys, I'm taking a new track. I'll be here again next Sunday and I want us to talk about advice to the young. You hear me at the back there? I'm a singer and a single mother and I'm feeling guilty about going on gigs and abandoning my daughter, so I'm writing this letter of confession which is turning out to be a letter of advice trying to explain life and the world to her, and perhaps you can help me, tell me if I've got it wrong. Next Sunday, OK?

SCENE 15

CLARE's BEDROOM

CHRISTOPHER and JASON, her sons, present.

CLARE: What am I to do with you? I have two sons I love who don't love each other. Will you never resolve your differences and agree about something worthwhile?

JASON: We have no differences, mother. Our mutual hatred is a fact. We agree on the existence of that fact.

CLARE: That's adolescent sophistry.

JASON: Not sophistry at all. My brother is an idiot who espouses dubious values and feeble arguments. Ask him what he thinks about the existence of evil.

CHRISTOPHER: I'm not going to engage mother in a discussion about something that doesn't exist.

JASON: Just explain how you arrive at that dainty conclusion about the non-existence of evil.

CHRISTOPHER: Oh, come on, Jason, let's not perform. She'll get upset and she's not strong enough.

JASON: She won't get upset. She should, but she won't because she loves you too much.

CLARE: I am here you know.

JASON: I just want you to understand why his stupidity attracts my contempt. Go on! Evil doesn't exist because… Finish it.

Waits.

Ok, I'll finish it then. Your oh so sweet and honest son thinks evil doesn't exist because – how does he put it? – because what we call an evil act is simply the act of creating a situation in which the perpetrator – now listen to this,

34

mother – in which the *perpetrator* is not suffering pain. An evil act is really, says your other son, an act of reassurance. The motive is benign. Do you get it, Mother? You want sophistry? There's sophistry for you: cruelty is an act of self-preservation. It's not that the wicked man wants to hurt others it's that he wants to reassure himself it is not him who is hurting.

CLARE: Christopher wants to think the best of people.

JASON: And in doing so becomes dangerously irresponsible.

CHRISTOPHER: OK. Now *you* explain what evil is and why you think it exists.

JASON: Evil is pleasure derived from another's pain. It delights in agony. Evil enjoys physical and mental agony, pure and simple. It seeks no self-justification, it offers no meek excuses. Unhappy childhoods play no part in evil, nor do cruel parents, or bullying siblings. It claims no psychological causes. Evil is inborn along with all other predilections to which heart and head are prone. Evil is evil, beyond reason or logic. Unadulterated!

CLARE: I prefer Christopher's more generous-spirited view.

JASON: They kidnapped a fifteen-year-old girl out of her house, mother, blind-folded her, raped and stabbed her and left her for dead. They were high neither on drink nor drugs, just high with the pleasure of it. Relieved, according to my brother, that it was not them being raped or stabbed. High on horror, as it were.

CLARE: What! What am I to do with you both?

SCENE 16

SPEAKERS' CORNER.

DEBATE.

DEBATOR: The last time I addressed you my theme was the cause of violence. I suggested that violence came from people who suspected their own stupidity. A type. A who-do-you-think-you-are? type. A think-you're-better-than-me type.

Let me tell you a little story. It took place when I was in secondary school. We were queuing up for lunch one day and there was this boy who took pleasure in taunting me. There was something about me that irritated him. What? God knows! I never found out what it was. It certainly wasn't my cleverness because I wasn't clever. I was bright and argumentative and risked writing essays that were not quite about the topic called for but my maths were mediocre, and I was merely OK in geography. History I enjoyed but science? Zero! So he didn't have to go into competition with me, there was nothing to compete with.

What I *did* possess was a quality of confidence. Don't ask me how but I gave the impression of being in control of my life and having a future. I was content and it got on this boy's nerves. So he was constantly looking for ways of baiting me, taunting me, putting me down; but nothing he did shook my confidence, my control never wavered. Drove him crazy.

So comes this lunchtime and we were in a queue and he approaches waving what looks like a black leather belt. But it's not. It's a length of liquorice – lickerish I used to think it was called. Remember it? It had grooves running down its length. And he says to me, this stocky, dark-haired little thug, he says: "Wanna taste a bit of my lickerish?" I don't like lickerish, I told him, and declined. He insisted: "Go on. Have a bite. Won't kill you." Again I declined repeating that I didn't like lickerish. The third time I declined he hit me. My earliest lesson in human behaviour. Violence employed against someone not sharing your tastes, beliefs or passions. Who do you think you are not to like what I like, not to believe what I believe? The desperate cry of the small mind, the insecure mind, the mean mind. Think you're better than me? Wham! Take that!

Types! The world is made up of types, ladies and gentlemen. They were seen knitting in Paris during the French Revolution as the guillotine fell. The same type kept guard over the Soviet gulags full of poets, politicians and professors who didn't like comrade Stalin's lickerish. The same type opened the doors of the gas chambers for those who refused un-kosher lickerish. And don't let us forget the so-called Chinese 'cultural revolution' and those little red-book-waving types who sent the cultured and educated classes to work and die in the countryside to show those cultured and educated classes what it was like to work manually. Who did they think they were to imagine intellectual life and artistic endeavour was *real* work? Eat my lickerish! You don't like my lickerish? Die!

I did not see Bin Laden as a Muslim, my friends, but as a type soured with failure – a type I call the murderous nothings of history who self-righteously fall in love with their own holiness, and contribute nothing to life but the destruction of stone Buddhas and beautiful tall towers and a taste for lickerish.

Next Sunday, ladies and gentlemen, I want us to talk about the flaws in ideology. Stay with me. We'll have a good time.

SCENE 17

SPEAKERS' CORNER.

LADY BETTY.

LADY B: 'My Lords, Ladies and Gentlemen. I had an aunt –
yes, even old women may once have had aunts – I had an
aunt who while burning at the stake – well not literally but
you know what I mean – said: "Betty" she said, "never be
chosen, never stand out in a crowd. If you have ideas keep
them to yourself, if you have opinions – suppress them.
Never argue with those in charge, those in authority, those
with power. Dress soberly, live modestly, don't shout or
become emotional or fall in love, if you have to fall in love
try to do it without passion. The majority," she said, "are
mediocre and filled with such venomous hatred of your joy
that they'll slice you into bloody little bloody bits of little
bloody pieces. Betty Lemon" she said, "keep your nose
clean and never be chosen."'

And what about those handicapped by fear of their priests?
Eh? What about them?

EXPLOSION

Snap blackout.

END OF PART ONE.

Part Two

SCENE 18

A RESTAURANT.

JASON and AMANDA at a table for two in a small, cosy restaurant.

JASON: Before Christopher comes to spoil you with a lavish birthday dinner let me –

AMANDA: You don't have to keep me company.

JASON: I don't have to but I want to, and besides I need you to list the fine qualities you see in my brother.

AMANDA: Why?

JASON: I don't love him but I want to.

AMANDA: You never will.

JASON: Let me try. List them!

AMANDA: Too many.

JASON: A few.

AMANDA: He has a rare capacity to love.

JASON: Love we know about, you make it obvious to us all.

AMANDA: But genuine love. I mean –

JASON: We believe you! But we're interested in what informs that love.

AMANDA: Me! I inform it.

JASON: Let's be precise about this. You're beautiful and intelligent. You can 'arouse' his love, but you're an outside element. What 'informs' his love comes from within him. I want to know what qualities you think he contains within him. (*Beat.*) I like your blue dress.

AMANDA: Joy. Joy informs his love – from his delight in other people's achievements to his smile. (*Referring to compliment.*) Thank you.

JASON: Personally I think he smiles too much. (*Beat.*) In fact I like everything about you.

AMANDA: How is it possible to smile *too* much?

JASON: I don't know but some people do.

AMANDA: And stop flirting with me.

JASON: Very little makes me smile so when I do my smile contains the full weight of my approval.

AMANDA: Not so! Your smile is of contempt, Jason, disdain.

JASON: You've always had good taste. Good taste and style rate high in my book.

AMANDA: There's joy in Christopher's smile never in yours.

JASON: The world mistrusts smilers, Amanda, especially joyful ones. I bet you don't know many people who like smilers.

AMANDA: Nonsense! Most people like smilers. Next time you're waiting for your doctor's appointment or your dentist's, count the patients who come through the door and smile.

JASON: Ugh! Nervous smiles.

AMANDA: Or walking in the street, for no reason, someone passes, catches your eye, and smiles.

JASON: I never return the smile.

AMANDA: How wretched of you.

JASON: I'd return yours.

AMANDA: Smilers light up a room.

JASON: Depress the pants off me. DOWN WITH SMILERS!

AMANDA: They're like salt, they bring out the taste of humanity.

JASON: Not for me. I want to hit a smiler, hurt him. Or her. DOWN WITH THEM!

AMANDA: Poor brother Christopher, having to live all these years with your bleak, theatrical misery.

JASON: DOWN WITH HAPPINESS! SEND THE HAPPY ONES HOME! BACK TO WHERE THEY CAME FROM!

AMANDA: I don't believe you, Jason, you just enjoy the role of naughty boy. The English have a weakness for naughty boys who outrage guests, get drunk at parties, swear loudly and shout at waiters. Middle-aged adolescents still shocking mummy and daddy who have long since died.

JASON: DOWN WITH SMILERS. A perfectly sound slogan. Think I'll organise a protest march around it.

AMANDA: Protesting against what for Christ's sake?

JASON: Too much gaiety in the world.

AMANDA: Not enough for my liking.

Enter CHRISTOPHER.

CHRISTOPHER: Happy birthday, darling.

He hands her a rose.

They embrace passionately.

JASON: And too much love while we're about it.

CHRISTOPHER: Imprison lovers, would you?

JASON: Not imprison them but ban displays in public.

AMANDA: No kissing 'hello' or 'goodbye'?

JASON: Save it for railway stations and departure lounges.

AMANDA: And dark alleys.

JASON: If you must.

> *AMANDA pulls CHRISTOPHER into a passionate embrace.*

AMANDA: I must! I must! Oh, how I must. Look at him – lips to be kissed, ears to be chewed, chest to be hugged and hung onto for dear life, for life with him *is* dear. Dear, dear, dear. And without him unimaginable.

JASON: The danger confronting lovers is to fall in love with themselves falling in love.

CHRISTOPHER: I've heard that before.

JASON: (*Singing.*)

> *Falling in love with love*
>
> *Is falling for make believe*

AMANDA: Don't you believe *any*thing is pure, untainted?

JASON: No! I doubt everything. (*Beat.*) On which note I take my leave.

> *Reaching for his wallet.*

There, I've kept her warm for you, Christopher. Allow me. Buy yourselves a bottle of birthday champagne and drink to love. It won't last!

CHRISTOPHER: But it seems there's room for crooners in your world?

JASON: Only those who croon about betrayal, mistaken choices, and hearts broken by the truth of things.

CHRISTOPHER: There's more than one truth about everything, dear brother.

JASON: Which is why everything should be doubted, dear brother.

> *Falling in love with love*
>
> *Is playing the fool....* (etc.)
>
> *Exit.*

AMANDA: My God your dear brother is depressing.

CHRISTOPHER: He's a hater. Hates everything and everyone, including himself. But he works hard not to show it. On the contrary he shows charm. People warm to him. He has the knack of humour, makes people laugh. But it's dark humour and cruel laughter, and people aren't aware of the cruelty until too late, and they leave his company feeling a strange mixture of pleasure and discomfort, and they vow never to spend time with him again. But they do. Despite themselves they're drawn to him. They can't turn down his invitations.

AMANDA: Because he's a good cook.

CHRISTOPHER: It helps.

AMANDA: Where did he learn that?

CHRISTOPHER: Our mother taught him – dicing, slicing, concocting, seasoning – came naturally. Not to me. Humour, charm...

AMANDA: A promising Independent parliamentary candidate and a good cook, to boot.

CHRISTOPHER: Irresistible! But I fear something.

AMANDA: Like what?

CHRISTOPHER: I fear violence lurking within him.

AMANDA: Charm hiding violence?

CHRISTOPHER: His charm is compensatory, not genuine; its roots reside in a wish to take revenge on nature.

AMANDA: Revenge for what?

CHRISTOPHER: He's interestingly ugly but he can't sustain a relationship.

AMANDA: Revenge for social inadequacy?

CHRISTOPHER: But he wants the world to believe his anger is on their behalf. Capitalism, he asserts, must be smashed before it can be rebuilt as something else.

AMANDA: What else?

CHRISTOPHER: Ah! The sixty thousand dollar question. He doesn't know. When we destroy the old the new will be revealed, he thinks. We can't abolish violence without violence.

AMANDA: That's a frightening thought. I've had it myself. There was this report came through the other day about a horrendous slaughter after a military take-over. Two hundred and fifty doctors, writers, teachers and professors. They all had their hands tied behind their backs and had been bayoneted, garrotted or shot. Imagine! The cream of intellectual life blotted out. Snap! Just like that.

CHRISTOPHER: Why are they always the first to go – poor bloody artists and intellectuals?

AMANDA: And I found myself wanting to murder the murderers, and I felt so ashamed.

CHRISTOPHER: We've all been hit that way.

AMANDA: But I have this dread of something even more awful about to happen. It's not a fear of the bomb, I don't think it's that, but some kind of anarchy. A break up of patterns of behaviour. I hoard things, which I fold away neatly in drawers. String and brown paper from parcels, and plastic bags – I've got three plastic bags full of plastic bags! And there's this cupboard full of imperishable goods – tins of soup, baked beans, stewed meat, packets of tea. Two weeks supply.

CHRISTOPHER: I've seen them, and wondered.

AMANDA: But that's not the kind of hoarding I really want to do. What I really want to do, and I'm ashamed to admit it, is dig a huge square hole somewhere, line it with cement and plastic, and fill it up with tins of vegetables and broths, jars of pickles and honey and salt and spices and sugar and flour and packets of candles and ground coffee and batteries and vacuum flasks and soaps and medicines and bandages... For what? A siege, perhaps? Some unspeakable disaster? God knows. I fear – I don't know – a time of aberration, a great lapse of human kindness. I fear old scores will be paid off and new injustices perpetrated. There are such mad angers about, and they frighten me and I want to lie low until they're spent.

Long pause.

CHRISTOPHER: I can't say enough times how much I love you. (*They kiss.*)

SCENE 19

SPEAKERS' CORNER.

COMEDY.

COMEDIENNE: I believe the world is divided between those who feel deeply and those who feel nothing.

Pause.

Anyone out there?

VOICE OFF: I believe the world is divided between the givers and the takers.

COMEDIENNE: Good! Very good! Now you all have to decide which you are – a giver or a taker.

SCENE 20

THE RESTAURANT.

CHRISTOPHER: FREYDA! Where is FREYDA? Why isn't anyone serving us? FREYDA!

Return to kissing.

SCENE 21

SPEAKERS' CORNER.

COMEDY.

VOICE OFF: What about a world divided between those joyful ones who have loved and those sad ones who have never loved?

COMEDIENNE: Excellent! Now, which are you – joyous or sad? Getting to understand the point of the game? Not as futile as it seemed, eh?

SCENE 22

RESTAURANT.

FREYDA appears.

FREYDA: Good evening, lovers. What can I get you to drink?

CHRISTOPHER: Champagne of course.

AMANDA: Even though it's from JASON.

CHRISTOPHER: We're celebrating her birthday.

AMANDA: And you! Just being with you.

FREYDA: Lovers! Lovers, lovers, lovers! I love lovers.

Gets champagne.

AMANDA: Another crazy romantic.

They embrace again.

Re-enter FREYDA with champagne.

FREYDA: Some people hate them, you know – lovers. Nothing drives them madder than to see two people kissing. Love's an affront. You ever thought about that? Love's an emotion so charged and pure that it can attract a pure and charged hatred. That's why I don't think lovers should love in public. Some people have murder in their eyes when they see lovers. And somewhere out there is a person so disappointed with their own life, so full of self-contempt that they're carrying murder in their pocket as well as in their eyes. A gun! To blow away lips that were blowing kisses. (*Imitates a gun.*) Pyeach! Pyeach! 'Put that tongue back in your mouth, lover!' Pyeach! Pyeach! 'Put those arms down by your sides, lover!' Pyeach! Pyeach! Wipe that shine from your eyes, lover! Who are you to be happy when I'm not?' Pyeach! Pyeach!

So drink up. Here you can hold hands, gaze at each other, touch and blow kisses. You're safe, lovers. Drink!

SCENE 23

SPEAKERS' CORNER.

COMEDY.

COMEDIENNE: I believe the world is divided between those who feel everything and those who feel nothing; those riven with guilts and those who are conscience-blind.

Come on now! Anymore voices out there? Play the game! You believe the world is divided how? How? How do you believe the world is divided? (*Beat.*) Christ! You're making me work hard for pennies.

V. OFF STAGE: (*Female.*) What about that problem with your daughter? You said you wanted help with a letter? That's why I'm here this Sunday. Sounded interesting.

COMEDIENNE: Right! How could I forget! Well I didn't. I just forgot I was going to share it with you. Thanks for reminding me.

Here's my problem – I'm a singer on the verge of giving up singing to try my hand at stand-up comedy, but no one thinks I'm very funny so I may have to stick with singing. I'm not a bad singer, in fact in certain quarters I've got a cult following. No, I'm not going to sing to you, you'll just have to take my word for it, but here's my dilemma: I'm also a single mother and I have this daughter, Juniper, who I feel guilty for neglecting when I go on gigs, so I'm writing a letter for her to read when she's fourteen. It started as a letter of apology for being a bad mum but it's turning into a letter of advice. So far I've advised her on four counts.

The fourth, and perhaps most important piece of advice, is about choosing her peers, and here's where I'd like *your* advice about *my* advice to my daughter. 'Select your peers,' I want to tell her. 'Don't go with the herd. Don't look to be one of the gang. I know there's great comfort in a gang,'

I want to tell her, 'in belonging, in being accepted but –
resist it! A gang,' I want to warn her, 'is made up of people
who are living their lives through each other'. I know!
I was part of a gang, one of the girls, always busy being
what I thought would please the others, picking up their
bad habits, thinking their thoughts, sharing their stupid
prejudices, laughing with them at their mindless hatreds.
We never questioned each other, we just raised our arms
and clenched our fists and stroked each other's nonsense,
terrified of stepping out of line. Not one of us had an
opinion that was our own. Not one of us was independent.
And we intimidated each other. If one of us dared to say 'I
don't agree! I don't think we should,' out would come that
dreary old cry: '*Who do you think you are?*'

I think I hate that cry more than any other in the whole
wide world, ladies and gentlemen. So I want to warn her:
If anyone cries it out to you, Juniper, you tell them: Juniper
thinks she's an individual! She thinks she can think her
own thoughts! She thinks she can rise above the herd! You
tell them that, sweetheart.

And then I change my mind. No! Don't, I should be telling
her. They'll slaughter you! Whatever you do, don't stand
above the herd. In fact don't even think of them as a herd.
They are *not* a herd, a herd is a collection of dumb animals.
They're not dumb animals. They're your (*Sardonically.*)
brothers and sisters, your comrades in arms, your link to
reality, your support system. I should be advising her to
stay with them, stay with them or they'll tear you limb
from limb.

Then I change my mind again. 'Take the risk!' I want to
yell. 'Stand out! Fly… Fly I want to advise her, don't join
the herd. Am I right? Should I be urging my only daughter
to take risks and fly, to stand out above the herd, the
crowd, the mob, go against the drift of things? Is the world

divided between the mob and the risk-takers? Is it? Tell me. I'm asking you.

EXPLOSION

SCENE 24

SPEAKERS' CORNER.

LADY BETTY.

LADY B: 'My Lords, Ladies and Gentlemen. I had a father – yes, even old women may once have had fathers – I had a father who advised me to be a writer and write rubbish. "Write rubbish" he advised, "write rubbish, make a fortune and keep us in our old age." But I didn't want to be a writer, not even one who made a fortune writing rubbish. I wanted to be, believe me or believe me not, a runner. Yes! Once I could run. Once I could swim, dive, the high jump, the long jump, leap over hurdles. An athlete! Joy! That's what *I* wanted to be my Lords, Ladies and Gentlemen, not a writer but a joyful runner who ran races. I was neither. I became a wife instead. To Sir James.

And what about those handicapped by marriage till death do them part, what about them, eh?

SCENE 25

CLARE's bedroom. Only AMANDA present.

JASON and CHRISTOPHER enter.

AMANDA: She's in the loo. Constipated.

CHRISTOPHER: Did you know the antiques shop had a bomb in it?

AMANDA: And I'm ashamed to confess that my only thought was – that's her birthday present gone.

JASON: No it's not. I collected it the day before the bombing.

CHRISTOPHER: You collected it the day before?

JASON: Fortunately!

CHRISTOPHER: Why then?

AMANDA: (*Dawning on her.*) Because he knew it was going to be bombed.

> *Ominous silence.*

You did didn't you? You knew it was going to be bombed.

JASON: I'd heard.

CHRISTOPHER: You're in with that group – The Anarchist Brigade.

AMANDA: The political crazies.

JASON: I most certainly am not. They're too feeble, too illiterate for me. Have you read the note they sent to *The Times*?

> *CHRISTOPHER lifts* The Times *from CLARE's bed.*

CHRISTOPHER: I've read it.

JASON: Read it again, out loud, and then tell me I could have been involved with such adolescent protest.

CHRISTOPHER: I can't. It offends my head.

> *AMANDA takes* The Times *from him and reads.*

AMANDA: *If you are not busy being born you are busy buying.* What does that mean 'busy being born'? If you're being born it's the woman who's busy – bearing you!

JASON: Read it! Read it!

AMANDA: (*Continuing.*) *In fashion as in everything else capitalists can only look backwards. The future is ours. Nothing to do except spend our wages on the latest skirt or shirt.* I can't go on. It doesn't make sense. (*Handing it to* CHRISTOPHER.) You finish it.

CHRISTOPHER: *Brothers, sisters, what are your real desires? Sit in the drug store, look distant, empty, bored or blow it up or burn it down.*

AMANDA: And who in the UK calls a chemist a drug store?

CHRISTOPHER: *You cannot reform profit, capitalism and inhumanity, just kick it till it breaks. Revolution!*

JASON: There! Can you associate me with such school playground crassness!

> *CLARE shuffles to her bed.*

CHRISTOPHER: So it was mere good fortune that you'd heard the bombing was going to take place?

JASON: Mere good fortune. But why, mother? Why this sentimental painting of old Jews dancing?

CLARE: I'll tell you the story, it's short and sweet. I was looking in my book of quotations for a pithy philosophical quote to put in Amanda's birthday card and I came across this instead.

> *She reaches for a book with a bookmark marking the place.*

> *She reads the quote.*

Men learned in the law came to the Besht – the founder of Hasidism – on an errand of dispute. 'In times gone by,' they protested, 'there were pious men in great numbers fasting from Sabbath to Sabbath, and inflicting their own bodies with self-devised torments. And now your disciples proclaim it, to all who care to listen, that much fasting is unlawful and self-torment a crime. Why?' The Besht answered, 'It is the aim and essence of my pilgrimage on earth to show my brethren by living demonstration how one may serve God with merriment and rejoicing. For he who is full of joy is full of love for people and all fellow creatures.'

And then as if by design, Christopher took me to lunch one day in that restaurant next to the antique shop and I saw this painting of dancing Hassids, and I knew in that instant what I wanted to look at from my bed, perhaps as I lay dying: dancing men serving their God with merriment and rejoicing. *For he who is full of joy is full of love for people and all fellow creatures.*

And now reassure me, Jason, you had nothing to do with the bombing of the antique shop in Hampstead.

JASON: Nothing!

CLARE: Swear!

JASON: I swear. (*Beat.*) But I can't swear I don't have some sympathy for their cause. Deprive people of their homes and land and they have no alternative but –

AMANDA: – but to blow up innocent people?

CLARE: Jan Pallack burned himself to death protesting against the Russian invasion of Czechoslovakia. Himself! Not other people. HIMSELF!

SCENE 26

SPEAKERS' CORNER.

DEBATE.

DEBATER: So what's the flaw in ideology? Take protest. Nothing wrong with protest. Sign of a healthy society. What goes wrong? I'll tell you what goes wrong. People! They fuck up protest. Start off wanting more democratic rights, end up wanting to overthrow democratic institutions.

Take politics. Nothing wrong with politics. It's the art of government. We have to be governed. Since Adam! So what goes wrong? I'll tell you what goes wrong. People! They become politicians, fuck up politics. Ambitious! Dishonest! Opportunist!

Take religion. Nothing wrong with wanting to believe in a God. Jesus! Buddha! Muhammad! Moses! They're all saying the same thing – be good, love one another, look after the kids! So what goes wrong? I'll tell you what goes wrong. People! Types! They become fanatics. Scream at one another. 'I'm holier than thou and all must be as holy as me!'

Types! Full of intoxicating hatreds handed down from father to son fucking up everything. Every fucking thing.

EXPLOSION

SCENE 27

CLARE's BEDROOM.

CHRISTOPHER, JASON, AMANDA present.

CLARE: Because I promise you this, Jason, if I discover before I die that you were mixed up with violent protest I would disown you.

JASON: No you wouldn't, mother.

CLARE: No, I wouldn't. But you'd send a deeply unhappy and disappointed woman to her grave.

JASON: I know I would, mother, so believe me. I am not linked to violent protest. But you want me to be honest, don't you? (*Beat.*) I understand violence.

CLARE: What do you understand? What is there to
understand?

JASON: Hatred! I understand hatreds.

CLARE: Hate is intoxicating.

AMANDA: I was at Speakers' Corner the other Sunday and one
of the speakers quoted a social worker in Northern Ireland
who described 'The Troubles' as the result of beery hatred
handed down from father to son.

JASON: Not all hatreds are beery hatreds.

CLARE: But they all *are* intoxicating.

JASON: Everyone needs something or someone to hate,
mother.

CLARE: Only as second best. People need someone or
something to revere as well.

JASON: It gets complicated, now. Reverence and hatred can go
hand in hand.

CLARE: One is healthy and one isn't.

JASON: It depends on the ends – if you revere justice it's
healthy to hate injustice.

CLARE: Providing *that* hate doesn't lead to a further injustice
which the violence can cause.

JASON: What if violence is the only means left to counter
injustice?

CHRISTOPHER: It never works. Violence is an ever downward
spiral that can't cease. Use violence and you set up a model
for the demagogues who follow you.

JASON: No! Use violence and the peace agreements follow.

CHRISTOPHER: No!

> *The rumble of the final explosion begins and grows through the next exchange reaching its climax by the end of the last BETTY LEMON speech in the next scene.*

Use violence and peace agreements full of compromise follow.

JASON: When was any peace agreement *not* compromised?

CHRISTOPHER: And when it's reached, up will rise the demagogues from your own ranks declaring the compromise has led to injustice and they'll call for violence asking as you've asked '*What if violence is the only means left to counter injustice?*' and they'll rise up as you once rose up, and they will become the new generation of so-called just men who will claim violence as *their* only means of achieving a true end to discontent and injustice…on and on and on ad absurdum.

AMANDA: And what about language and music as a means of protest against injustice?

JASON: The arts?

CHRISTOPHER: The poet and the singer!

JASON: Down with them! Soften resolve, present too many sides.

AMANDA: Right! Subversive!

JASON: Distracting!

AMANDA: Many sides!

JASON: DOWN WITH THE ARTS!

CHRISTOPHER: Confusing!

JASON: Yes! DOWN WITH THEM!

SCENE 28

SPEAKERS' CORNER.

LADY BETTY.

LADY B: 'My Lords, Ladies and Gentlemen. I had a mother –
yes, even old women may once have had mothers – I had
a mother, a strong and tiny thing she was who gave me one
piece of advice I never forgot. "Talk" she said. "Always *say*
it. Something is remembered."

> *The rumbling grows.*

> *BETTY repeats –*

…a strong and tiny thing she was who gave me one piece
of advice I never forgot. "Talk," she said. "Always *say* it.
Something is remembered."

> *The rumbling grows.*

…"Talk," she said. "Always *say* it. Something is
remembered."

> *The rumbling approaches climax.*

…"Always *say* it. Something is remembered.

> *The rumbling reaches a climax.*

…"Something is remembered."

> *EXPLOSION*

> *END.*